TRIANGLES
FOR
TWO

**Failures in
Communication**

**Three Plays by
David Wiltse**

S A M U E L   F R E N C H , I N C.
45 West 25th Street   NEW YORK, N.Y. 10010
7623 Sunset Boulevard   HOLLYWOOD 90046
LONDON   *TORONTO*

ISBN 0 573 62764 9   Printed in U.S.A.   #22221

IMPORTANT BILLING AND CREDIT REQUIREMENTS

All producers of TRIANGLES FOR TWO: FAILURES IN COMMUNICATION (TO WIT AND TO WHOM, OTIS PROPOSES and TRIANGLES FOR TWO) *must* give credit to the Author of the Plays in all programs distributed in connection with performances of the Plays and in all instances in which the titles of the Plays appear for purposes of advertising, publicizing or otherwise exploiting the Plays and/or a production. The name of the Author *must* also appear on a separate line, on which no other name appears, immediately following the titles, and *must* appear in size of type not less than fifty percent the size of the title type.

TRIANGLES FOR TWO

These plays take place on the same set,
a neutral space to represent a living room in a middle class suburb.
The set décor will change only minimally —
different pictures or throw pillows, for instance.
The plays will be performed by the same two actors.
It is recommended that they be presented without intermission.

The connections among the three plays in time and circumstance
should not be pondered too literally.
A bit of confusion is perfectly acceptable.

IMPORTANT BILLING AND CREDIT REQUIREMENTS

All producers of TRIANGLES FOR TWO: FAILURES IN COMMUNICATION (TO WIT AND TO WHOM, OTIS PROPOSES and TRIANGLES FOR TWO) *must* give credit to the Author of the Plays in all programs distributed in connection with performances of the Plays and in all instances in which the titles of the Plays appear for purposes of advertising, publicizing or otherwise exploiting the Plays and/or a production. The name of the Author *must* also appear on a separate line, on which no other name appears, immediately following the titles, and *must* appear in size of type not less than fifty percent the size of the title type.

TRIANGLES FOR TWO

These plays take place on the same set,
a neutral space to represent a living room in a middle class suburb.
The set décor will change only minimally —
different pictures or throw pillows, for instance.
The plays will be performed by the same two actors.
It is recommended that they be presented without intermission.

The connections among the three plays in time and circumstance
should not be pondered too literally.
A bit of confusion is perfectly acceptable.

TO WIT AND TO WHOM

(SCENE: The living room of a suburban upper middle class home. Entrance from bedrooms on one side, entrance from outdoors and kitchen on the other.)

(AT RISE: HUSBAND enters from kitchen, holding newspaper. He saunters past a spot of moisture on the floor, looks down speculatively. A bath towel lies beside it. One slipper is a few feet away. The belt of a bathrobe is a few feet away in the other direction. In his mind, HUSBAND reconstructs the event that caused this litter then crosses to chair, sits, opens the newspaper. Pause. WIFE enters from bedroom dressed in bathrobe and one slipper, crosses to spot on floor, picks up the bathrobe belt, puts it on, slips on the other slipper and uses towel to clean the spot. She does not see HUSBAND who watches her silently.)

HUSBAND. *(Pause)* Reading here about a man who put his wife through a wood chipper.

WIFE. *(Startled)* You startled me!

HUSBAND. Did I?

WIFE. Yes! That sort of thing is awfully rude.

HUSBAND. What sport of thing?

WIFE. Slipping up behind one. Barking at one.

HUSBAND. Barking, was I? I thought of it as conversational in tone.

WIFE. It would have been conversational in tone if we were having a conversation. As we weren't it had the same effect as barking. I didn't know you were here.

HUSBAND. That would account for it.

WIFE. What?

HUSBAND. Being startled. Sudden discovery of the husband, bound to do it.

WIFE. You're home early.

5

HUSBAND. Not really.

WIFE. It's noon.

HUSBAND. I didn't go to work.

WIFE. I thought you did.

HUSBAND. Did you?

WIFE. Yes. I thought you'd gone.

HUSBAND. Strange.

WIFE. That is what you do. That's your routine. You get up in the morning and go to work. That's your routine.

HUSBAND. Not all that regularly.

WIFE. You're a creature of habit in that regard. Morning comes and off you go.

HUSBAND. Must be boring for you to watch. Must be tedious.

WIFE. Not at all. I rather count on it.

HUSBAND. Predictable, I would say.

WIFE. Dependable.

(Pause)

HUSBAND. Bit of trouble for you? Spot of inconvenience?

WIFE. Not at all, glad to see you.

HUSBAND. I mean the floor.

WIFE. Ah.

HUSBAND. Standing there dripping, were you? Just dripping and dripping?

WIFE. Looking out the window. Thinking.

HUSBAND. Thinking of me?

WIFE. Thinking of you?

HUSBAND. Were you? At all?

WIFE. When?

HUSBAND. As you stood there, looking out the window. Thinking. Dripping.

WIFE. Was I thinking of you and dripping?

HUSBAND. I don't know. That's why I ask. In the spirit of inquiry.

WIFE. No. Not actually.

HUSBAND. Ah.

WIFE. I had thought of you earlier, though.

HUSBAND. That should be enough. Wouldn't want to overdo.

WIFE. Just not while I was dripping.

HUSBAND. *(Pause)* I notice a bit of a mark in the floor there.

WIFE. Really?

HUSBAND. What do you suppose that's from?

WIFE. This mark?

HUSBAND. What do you suppose that's from?

WIFE. I have no idea.

HUSBAND. Looks rather like a spur mark.

WIFE. A spur mark?

HUSBAND. Wearing spurs, were you?

WIFE. When?

HUSBAND. As you stood there, dripping.

WIFE. Why would I wear spurs?

HUSBAND. Better purchase, I suppose.

WIFE. You're thinking of crampons.

HUSBAND. Am I?

WIFE. Much better purchase with crampons. Not spurs.

HUSBAND. Good Lord, you're right. It must have been crampons. Why would you be standing by the window in spurs? *(Pause)* What were you thinking?

WIFE. When?

HUSBAND. When you were thinking of me.

WIFE. I thought you meant when I was looking out the window.

HUSBAND. No, no.

(Pause. WIFE thinks, HUSBAND waits. WIFE stops thinking and cleans up the mess.)

WIFE. What did you bark at me when I came in?

HUSBAND. Ah. Reading here about a man who put his wife through a wood chipper.

WIFE. I don't believe it.

HUSBAND. Newspaper is taking that position.

WIFE. Seems hardly likely.

HUSBAND. The *Times* is quite adamant.

WIFE. Why, do you suppose?

HUSBAND. Apparently he had certain dissatisfactions.

WIFE. I don't imagine she was too pleased, either.

HUSBAND. Read about it, have you?

WIFE. Of course not.

HUSBAND. No ... seems there was a lover.

WIFE. Hers or his?

HUSBAND. Hers? How interesting you would think that.

WIFE. Why?

HUSBAND. The usual reasons for taking a lover, I suppose. Lust, cosmic destiny, unspeakable boredom, that sort of thing.

WIFE. Why interesting that I would think she took a lover? Women do.

HUSBAND. Do they? I thought only men did that.

WIFE. Whom do you think men take for lovers?

HUSBAND. You're quite right, of course, but still one finds it so annoying when you start a sentence with whom.

WIFE. Was she dead?

HUSBAND. When?

WIFE. When he put her through the chipper.

HUSBAND. At some point in the process, bound to be.

(Pause. He returns to paper, she to mess.)

WIFE. Strange.

HUSBAND. Hum?

WIFE. *He* was having the affair?

HUSBAND. Who?

WIFE. The man with the chipper.

HUSBAND. So the *Times* would have us believe. Hard to credit, but there it is.

WIFE. Very strange.

HUSBAND. Where are the old values, eh? Time was, a fellow wanted a bit of sexual diversion, he'd turn to the wife. Nowadays, of course, she's having none of it ... Or not with her husband, at any rate.

WIFE. Why didn't she put *him* through the wood chipper?

HUSBAND. She was hardly in a condition to do so, having just been through it herself. He did think of it first, after all. She who hesitates and so forth.

WIFE. There's a lesson there, isn't there?

HUSBAND. Is there?

WIFE. I think so. *(Pause)* Did he expect to get away with it?

HUSBAND. Oh, I should imagine. Say she's run away from home, people claim to see her at shopping malls over the years. The usual.

WIFE. So you never left the house at all, then?

HUSBAND. No. Not at all.

WIFE. Funny.

HUSBAND. Mildly amusing, perhaps ...

WIFE. Funny that you didn't answer the phone.

HUSBAND. It rang, did it?

WIFE. Rang and rang. Finally the answering machine took it.

HUSBAND. Hard to imagine life without those machines, isn't it?

WIFE. Not particularly.

HUSBAND. No, I suppose not.

WIFE. It was a woman.

HUSBAND. Oh, yes?

WIFE. The same woman who calls you and hangs up when I answer. *(Pause)* She didn't leave a message.

HUSBAND. Busy, were you?

WIFE. When?

HUSBAND. When the phone rang and rang.

WIFE. I was standing by the window, thinking.

HUSBAND. Not of me, though.

WIFE. No, I'd already done that.

HUSBAND. *(Pause)* If she didn't leave a message, how did you know it was a woman?

WIFE. You're not having an affair with a man, are you?

HUSBAND. Certainly not. What a suggestion. *(Pause)* Still, a lot of that going around. Men at the station wearing clamps on their nipples under business suits, waiting for the eight-oh-three. *(Pause)* Where are the old values, eh? *(Pause)* How odd you would think that.

WIFE. I didn't.

HUSBAND. Still.

WIFE. *(Pause)* Is she anyone I know?

HUSBAND. I can't say. Her husband is an airline pilot.

WIFE. Does he know?

HUSBAND. Know what?

WIFE. His wife is having an affair.

HUSBAND. Is she, by God? I didn't realize.

WIFE. *(Pause)* Whom are you talking about?

HUSBAND. The lady who went through the chipper.

WIFE. Ah … I wasn't.

HUSBAND. Ah. *(Pause)* Are you sure "Whom are you talking about" is the right construction? Seems — infelicitous.

WIFE. Felicity isn't everything in life.

HUSBAND. Quite right … Nor grammar, I suppose.

WIFE. Is she a good deal younger?

HUSBAND. Who?

WIFE. The woman on the phone.

HUSBAND. The one who doesn't speak?

WIFE. Is she a good deal younger?

HUSBAND. Younger than who? … *(Finishing the word whom.)* mmm.

WIFE. Me, for instance.

HUSBAND. I, isn't it? *(Pause)* Younger than I? You would know.

WIFE. Yes, younger than I. You were right.

HUSBAND. Oh, good.

WIFE. *(Pause)* Is she?

(HUSBAND returns to his newspaper, does not answer. After a pause, WIFE opens her robe to him, revealing herself. He slowly lowers newspaper, studies her.)

HUSBAND. Yes, I'd say so.

(WIFE closes her robe.)

HUSBAND. How's it going with the gardener? What's his name? Roger? How's it going with Roger?

WIFE. His name is Richard. But you know that.

HUSBAND. Why do you suppose I thought of Roger?

WIFE. His name is Richard (Dicky Bananas) Caputo.

HUSBAND. Oh, yes, I do remember. Dicky Bananas. Strange name for parents to give a child, don't you think? "What shall we name the little darling, sweetheart? Oh, how about Dicky Bananas?"

WIFE. I believe he was named for his godfather.

HUSBAND. Oh, a family name. Well, that explains it.

WIFE. You should remember his name, you hired him, after all.

HUSBAND. Did I? I suppose I did. Of course it wasn't his name I was most interested in at the time.

WIFE. In what were you interested?

HUSBAND. I was interested in his gardening skills, of course.

WIFE. Yes.

HUSBAND. And other things.

WIFE. Of course. You were interested in his other things.

HUSBAND. No Johnny One Note, he.

WIFE. I should say not.

HUSBAND. He's developed into something more than just a gardener, after all, hasn't he?

WIFE. Oh, yes.

HUSBAND. His other skills have come in handy.

WIFE. Very handy.

HUSBAND. His way with the oboe, for instance. Those glorious solos, Mozart, Boccherini, Brahms. Plaintive tones, evocative sonorities, sweet, doleful music wafting up from the hydrangea and the snowball bush. Must say I envy you. All that mawkish gawp.

WIFE. He doesn't play the oboe.

HUSBAND. Doesn't he? I was certain he had a hobby.

WIFE. He shoots.

HUSBAND. Every man needs a hobby.

WIFE. He's very devoted to it.

HUSBAND. I don't think there's ever been a really first class solo oboist name Bananas. Not a really first class one.

WIFE. There's a good deal more to him than is readily apparent.

HUSBAND. Delighted to hear it. And you're getting on well, are you?

WIFE. Oh, yes. I'm getting to know him. He's revealing himself layer by layer. *(Pause)* Like an onion.

HUSBAND. What does he shoot?

WIFE. He hasn't told me yet.

HUSBAND. Still more secrets to learn?

WIFE. Oh, yes. Richard has more levels than a parking garage. You should get to know him. You should talk to him. The two of you should converse. You would find him delightful.

HUSBAND. I'm sure of it.

WIFE. You should solicit his opinions on various matters. How he feels about humus. The value of the earthworm in oxygenating the soil. You would be edified.

HUSBAND. How does he feel about the efficacy of wood chips as compost? Do you know at all? Have you discussed chips with him? Or has he been too busy with his oboe?

WIFE. He's never too busy for me. *(Pause)* You should get to know him better. You could learn from him.

HUSBAND. Actually, I had a bit of a chat with him today. Nothing deep. No philosophy. Just a chat.

WIFE. Really?

HUSBAND. Not a chinfest. Not a palaver. Just a chat. *(Pause)* I asked him how he came to be standing naked in front of the window, dripping onto the floor.

WIFE. Did he have his oboe?

HUSBAND. No, he was naked. Except for his spurs.

WIFE. Not really naked then.

HUSBAND. Well ... Principally.

WIFE. Strange.

HUSBAND. I thought so.

WIFE. Where do you suppose his oboe had got to?

HUSBAND. I had the impression he had already used it.

WIFE. I hope you didn't embarrass him.

HUSBAND. I?

WIFE. Walking in on him, semi-naked.

HUSBAND. I was fully clothed, actually. *(Pause)* I said to him, Richard Dickie Bananas, what are you doing?

WIFE. You asked him, then.

HUSBAND. I wanted to know. It's my house. My living room. My view ... Well, perhaps not my view, exactly, God's view, but certainly my window. Naturally I was curious why a complete stranger was standing naked in my living room usurping God's view. Do you feel I was too proprietary?

WIFE. He wasn't a complete stranger, of course. You hired him.

HUSBAND. I didn't hire him to drip. I hired him for matters horticultural. Besides, I didn't recognize him.

WIFE. You didn't recognize him. Even though you hired him? This man with whom you confer daily by the hydrangeas?

HUSBAND. You exaggerate.

WIFE. Daily confabs. I count on them. Up in the morning, off to work, home in the evening, out in the yard for a whispering discussion by the hedge, blue cigar smoke rising. I set my watch by these things. What do you discuss every day with this man whom you don't recognize in your own house?

HUSBAND. Agronomy.

WIFE. I am surprised you didn't recognize him.

HUSBAND. It's one thing to recognize a man by your hedge, quite another to know him naked in your living room.

WIFE. Who did you think he was?

HUSBAND. Not whom?

WIFE. Certainly not.

HUSBAND. I assumed he was a friend of yours.

WIFE. Standing naked? Why would a friend of mine be standing naked by the window?

HUSBAND. Couldn't imagine. That's why I asked him.

WIFE. What did he say?

HUSBAND. Said he had just taken a shower.

WIFE. There you are then.

HUSBAND. I said to myself, "he's very clean." Sudsing up in the middle of the day. Hosing down at noon. That's cleanly to a fault. Must be a fetish. Must hamper his work. Dashing off to the shower every whip stitch. Who's minding the garden while all this ablution is going on? What about the price of soap?

WIFE. You seemed to get quite worked up over the matter.

HUSBAND. Not at all. I scarcely thought about it.

WIFE. Does she ever speak of me?

HUSBAND. Who?

WIFE. The woman on the phone. When you're together. When you're panting together, when you've thrust your tongue in her ear, does she ever speak of me?

HUSBAND. Seems I misjudged him. It wasn't a fetish at all. He had gasoline on his clothes. He came in the house to get the gasoline off.

WIFE. Or afterwards, when you're lying together, when she's braiding the hair on your chest into little knots, does she ask about me?

HUSBAND. He says you told him to take his clothes off.

WIFE. I didn't want him to explode.

HUSBAND. I don't actually have that much hair on my chest.

WIFE. Don't you?

HUSBAND. No ... Not for knotting. I have scarcely any hair on my chest at all. I have a body like porcelain.

WIFE. I must have been thinking of something else.

HUSBAND. You have often remarked upon it. You have said — admiringly — that I have skin like fine china.

WIFE. Perhaps I said that *I* have skin like fine china.

HUSBAND. You said that *I* have skin like fine china.

WIFE. And that's what I meant.

HUSBAND. *(Pause)* Is he a Buddhist, by any chance?

WIFE. Who?

HUSBAND. Roger.

WIFE. *(Pause)* Dick.

HUSBAND. Given to self-immolation, is he? Protesting something in the inimitable Buddhist fashion?

WIFE. I believe he's a Unitarian. *(Pause)* I could be wrong. I've never asked. *(Pause)* I've sensed it.

HUSBAND. Do Unitarians set themselves alight?

WIFE. Occasionally, I suppose. Why not?

HUSBAND. *(Pause)* Don't think of them in that way. Unitarians in their saffron robes torching themselves for justice in Tibet. *(Pause)* And you stopped him, didn't you?

WIFE. Stopped him?

HUSBAND. From immolating himself.

WIFE. Was he going to immolate himself?

HUSBAND. Why else would he douse himself with gasoline?

WIFE. I believe he spilled the gasoline while filling the backhoe.

HUSBAND. Ah. *(Pause)* So little self-sacrifice these days. I recall the time when men were lighting up for their principles at the drop of a placard. Where are the old values, where are they now, eh?

WIFE. I don't believe Roger has any principles. He works for money. He told me he works strictly for cash.

HUSBAND. A rather great deal of cash, actually. Rather too much for him to be taking showers on the job.

WIFE. Is it a big job?

HUSBAND. Which?

WIFE. The one you hired him to do. The one you're paying him rather a great deal of cash to perform. The one you confer about down by the hedge.

HUSBAND. Big job? *(Pause)* Not big, but important.

WIFE. He must be flattered, being hired for such an important job.

HUSBAND. He hasn't said. He doesn't talk much. Perhaps you've noticed.

WIFE. He talks to me.

HUSBAND. Does he?

WIFE. He talks rather a lot to me. He has had a great deal to say to me. He fairly rattles on in my presence.

HUSBAND. *(Pause)* I've found him quite mute.

WIFE. He has banter with me. Repartee.

HUSBAND. Really? I'm quite surprised. When do you have these talks? Not when he's playing his oboe, surely. Surely not.

WIFE. When he's taking his shower.

HUSBAND. Ah.

WIFE. And afterwards. When he's drying. When he's standing by the window, drying, and the water is running off his body in rivulets and streams, and coursing off his limbs in great surging rivers and cascades, and pouring from his trunk and raging floods and oceans … And when he dries his chest, that hairy chest, that rain forest of hair, that machete-thick Matto Grosso of hair sprouting and curling and craning upwards from the broad plain of his chest as if from the jungle floor, fetid and damp and rising, lifting, soaring up and up from that great hirsute hormone-oozing, pheremone-reeking primal monolithic steaming brute of a man.

HUSBAND. *(Pause)* Are you quite sure you have the right man?

WIFE. Right for what?

HUSBAND. Are we speaking of the same man? This chap who showers and drips, this jungle dwelling brute of a man with the spurs — is he the same man I confer with whom by the snowball bush? *(Pause)* Because I sense a dissimilarity in your description. *(Pause)* Did you notice any distinguishing marks?

WIFE. Do you mean scars?

HUSBAND. Not only scars, not just scars, no. This dripping floor-flooder of yours who might or might not be the cigar puffing hedge trimmer, does he happen to sport a small tattoo?

WIFE. Yes, he does.

HUSBAND. Very high on the inner thigh?

WIFE. Quite high.

HUSBAND. *(Pause)* A scene from Brueghel of drunken peasants, about the size of a dime, bordered with an indecipherable script?

WIFE. *(Pause)* It's in Italian. "Come e ecco!" Or, loosely, "how about that!"

HUSBAND. *(Pause)* Right thigh?

WIFE. Left thigh.

HUSBAND. He has deceived you. You have the wrong man. *(HUSBAND stands by window, looking out.)* What is he doing with the backhoe?

WIFE. *(Joining him.)* Digging a hole.

HUSBAND. It's quite a large hole. *(Pause)* I remember a time when it would take a man a day to dig a hole that deep. One man, one shovel. A great deal of dirt. Pounds and pounds, I should think. Back-breaking work, of course. Mindless, thankless, brute dumb labor without craft or appreciation. At mid-day one would rest beside it, dangling one's feet into the abyss, perhaps, eating a dried salami and drinking filthy red wine. Staring vacantly into the emptiness one had wrought, brain-dead, sweating like an ox, reeking of garlic and superstition. Then, bottle down, wipe the grease from your face and back to it with a purpose. Still, when one was finished, one had a hole. One could stand on the edge and look down and say, "now there's a space with nothing in it. And I'm responsible for it. Were it not for me, that hole would not exist." *(Pause)* If a hole can be said to exist. Being an exercise in emptiness, as it were ... Still, those were the days. Where have they gone, eh? Today any hired gunman can scoop out a hole with a backhoe in minutes and never reflect on the thing philosophically.

WIFE. Still, *you* can reflect on it.

HUSBAND. Yes, *I* can reflect on it, but I can hardly be expected to tour the countryside, reflecting on everyone else's hole. It's not my job, is it? I have other things to do ... And what happens when I'm gone? *(Pause)* That is quite a large hole.

WIFE. Six feet.

HUSBAND. I'd call that quite large.

WIFE. It depends what you put in it. If you put a grand piano in it, for instance, it would be quite a small hole. It would be an altogether insufficient hole. It would scarcely serve a hole-like purpose at all.

HUSBAND. What is a hole-like purpose?

WIFE. That rather depends where the hole is placed. The purpose of a hole in the wall, for instance, would be fenestration.

HUSBAND. I was referring to a hole in the ground. What would be the hole-like purpose of a hole in the ground? ... Generally ... Theoretically ... If you know.

WIFE. *(Pause)* Concealment. Interment. Entombment ... Burial.

HUSBAND. What do you suppose Richard Dicky Bananas is going to bury, inter or conceal in that six foot hole?

WIFE. You, perhaps?

HUSBAND. Me?

WIFE. A yew tree. Perhaps he's going to plant a yew tree.

HUSBAND. Surely you're mistaken ... A yew is a shrub, not a tree.

WIFE. Is it?

HUSBAND. Oh, yes.

WIFE. Are you certain?

HUSBAND. I'd stake my life on it.

WIFE. *(Pause)* As you wish.

HUSBAND. *(Pause)* I am more than six feet.

WIFE. Are you?

HUSBAND. Oh, yes. Considerably.

WIFE. Really?

HUSBAND. I am a great deal longer than six feet. It would be a mistake to think otherwise.

WIFE. How long are you?

HUSBAND. I am six feet and four inches.

WIFE. You don't look it.

HUSBAND. I carry it well. It is well distributed. My proportions are classical.

WIFE. I would have said you were a smaller man.

HUSBAND. No, no.

WIFE. If anyone had inquired about your length, I would have said six feet or less.

HUSBAND. That would have been a serious mistake. *(Pause)* You, on the other hand, are less than six feet.

WIFE. Does that include the root ball?

HUSBAND. *(Pause)* I am astounded. I am perplexed. To discover after all these years that you have a root ball. Why have I never noticed?

WIFE. Perhaps you never bothered to look. Perhaps you took things for granted. Perhaps there was a great deal going on beneath the surface that you never took into consideration when making your observations.

HUSBAND. You shock me. Such an accusation.

WIFE. Perhaps all of your calculations are wrong. Perhaps you have misjudged everything.

HUSBAND. *(At window.)* He has finished digging the hole.

WIFE. Time to plant yew.

HUSBAND. He's coming towards the house.

WIFE. Perhaps he's coming for another shower. He quite enjoyed the last one.

HUSBAND. He has no more time for showers. He has all that

wood to chip. That's why he was hired. That's why I'm paying him all that money.

WIFE. Maybe he's coming to play his oboe.

HUSBAND. There's no time for that. I'm paying him cash.

WIFE. Perhaps he prefers art to commerce.

HUSBAND. *(Pause)* Perhaps.

(Together they watch the gardener come towards the house, slowly turning their heads to face the door where he will enter as ...)
(Slow fade to black.)

THE END

OTIS PROPOSES

(SCENE: The same set as in the previous play. It is now KATE's apartment.)

(AT RISE: KATE is at coffee table, editing a manuscript. She is wearing Walkman earphones. Doorbell rings, she does not hear it, continues to work. Bell rings again, pause, knock on the door. Another pause. OTIS enters, peering about.)

OTIS. Hello? Kate? Ah, there you are. Looking pretty as a picture, good enough to eat, a sight for sore eyes.

(KATE still has not noticed him. She speaks to the manuscript, attacks it with a pencil.)

KATE. Redundant.

OTIS. Yes, well. Could be, could be. Still, a harsh greeting.

KATE. *(Seeing him. Screams.)* Otis!

OTIS. Good God, where! Oh, you mean me.

KATE. I didn't hear you come in.

OTIS. Slipped in quiet as a — uh — uh — I know the word, don't help. What is that thing that slips in? Quiet as a — uh — uh ... Silent as — uh — oh — it's a carol, you know it. *(He hums "Oh come all ye faithful.)* Ta ta tata ta ta.

KATE. Otis?

OTIS. Yes, my dear?

KATE. What on earth are you talking about?

OTIS. Haven't a clue. Something musical, was it?

KATE. Sit down, Otis. Would you like something to drink?

OTIS. Wouldn't want to put you to any trouble.

KATE. It's no trouble, I'll just pour it. What would you like?

OTIS. If you insist. Perhaps a crème de menthe frappe.

21

KATE. *(Gives him a look.)* I'll see what I can do. I'll just be a minute.

(KATE exits. OTIS stands, mutters to himself for a moment, rehearsing what he had planned to say. Then, for practice, he sinks to one knee, taking ring box from his pocket in one hand, stretching the other towards the imaginary Kate in the classic position of a marriage proposal.)

OTIS. Introductory remarks, yattada yattada, a few endearments, list of my virtues — take a while, that, hah-hah – perhaps, an anecdote, no no, straight to the point. In short my dear, would you do me the very great honor of becoming ...
KATE. *(O.S.)* What?
OTIS. *(Startled)* What?

(KATE pokes head in.)

KATE. What?
OTIS. What?
KATE. What did you say? I didn't hear you.
OTIS. Didn't hear me?
KATE. I heard you. I didn't understand you. But then that's often the case ... What are you doing on the floor?
OTIS. Ahhh — noticed a bit of a mark here. Gouge, really. Looks like a golf divot, I'd say. Practice in the house, do you?
KATE. That was here when I moved in. It looks like spur marks to me.
OTIS. I would have said an eight iron. Had a bit of a problem like that at home myself. Carpet's the answer. Ceiling's too low for a full driver, but if you choke down on a wedge ...
KATE. I'll get your drink.

(KATE exits. OTIS tries to rise, but his joints are locked in position. He tries to pull himself off one knee with his hands, scoots along the floor a bit on one knee, finally manages to get himself into a chair just as KATE enters.)

KATE. Here you are. Is mineral water all right?

OTIS. Perfect.

KATE. Are you okay? You look a little flushed.

OTIS. In the pink.

KATE. Before we go to dinner, Otis, I absolutely have to finish editing this story Carter wrote about the illegal golf ball. I promised Shep I'd have it for him first thing in the morning. You don't mind, do you?

OTIS. Right you are, business first.

KATE. You'll forgive me if I wear these? It helps me to concentrate. It's a tape of the Ganges River. In India?

OTIS. Holy river, monks in breech-cloths bathing themselves. All that time in the water but the odor on these chaps. Try a little soap, swami. That the Ganges you mean?

KATE. *(Cooly)* This is where the river runs through Benares. Where Yogi Hatchhadanandaramasamalama lives and teaches.

OTIS. Reincarnation, karma, all that yoga twaddle. Spend a bad life, come back as a cockroach, isn't that it?

KATE. Or a publisher.

OTIS. What? Oh, yes, a publisher, me you mean, ha-ha. Well, still, the thing is, live like a swine, come back as a bug, all very well so far, no argument there, but then what, eh? How do you get back to human again? Perform good works when you've got six legs? It would take all your concentration just to walk.

KATE. *(Stifling her annoyance.)* Still, some of us like it. *(Of earphones.)* I'll just put it on, then, all right? I can still hear you.

(KATE puts on earphones, looks at the manuscript.)

OTIS. You can hear me then?

KATE. *(Removes earphones.)* What?

OTIS. You can hear me all right with those on?

KATE. Oh, yes.

(Puts them on.)

OTIS. Saw a man drive off with a wood chipper when I arrived.

Thought for a moment he came from here. Must have been next door. Make a dreadful racket, those machines. Sounds like something screaming.

KATE. What?

OTIS. Chipper?

KATE. Not bad, thank you.

(Returns to manuscript.)

OTIS. I read that article Carter wrote about the illegal ball. Damned good. Fine man, Carter, fine man. Bit of a hormone problem, of course. Willing to rut with a flagpole. Still, excellent writer.

KATE. *(Not hearing him.)* Carter's a moron.

OTIS. He has that one drawback. Although, in a writer, one must say, nothing surprising there. Still, Carter does overdo. I saw him making a play for what's her name? The girl in accounting? You know, the one with the hairy legs? Woman absolutely refuses to shave. Her choice, of course, still and all, come summer and the tank tops, one hopes she doesn't hail a cab. Still, Carter doesn't seem to mind. Of course the man requires little more sexual stimulus than a pulse beat. He did seem to be making some headway, I must say. She was looking at him as moon-faced as — well — the moon.

KATE. *(Removes earphones.)* What are you talking about?

OTIS. Oh, that young woman, what's her name, you know her name, you have lunch with her, name of an animal, what's it called? Not a zebra, nothing like a zebra, that's not it, but it's close. More like the other thing, see here, on the savannah, bounding about *(On his feet.)* bounding, bounding.

KATE. Main?

OTIS. Mane? You're thinking of a lion. See here, picture this, darkest Africa. Serengeti plains, elephants, crocodiles, what not, then here they come, bounding, bounding — oh, come on! Famous bounders! What do you call them? King Solomon's Mines, Deborah Kerr crouched behind a tree trunk, forest fire in the distance or something, who's to say, then here they come, vast quantities of them, bounding, bounding, right over the tree trunk, right over Deb, thought I'd die from excitement. From there straight to the beach and Burt

Lancaster, very sexy that, pawing each other in the waves. Beautiful woman, love of my youth. Wonder what became of her? Bit long in the tooth, now, I suppose.

KATE. Otis?

OTIS. Yes, my dear.

KATE. What are you talking about?

OTIS. That girl from accounting. Giselle. Thought I told you.

KATE. Why are you talking about Giselle?

OTIS. Just remarking that Carter and she, she and Carter, bit of a thing going on there, bit of an item.

KATE. I don't think so.

OTIS. Oh, yes. Things heating up there, trysts in the copy room, so on.

KATE. I believe you're wrong.

(OTIS lays a finger beside his nose, then points it upward.)

OTIS. Time will tell.

KATE. Otis, listen to me. There is no truth to that rumor. Carter is not interested in her. Take my word for it.

OTIS. Best speak to Carter about that.

KATE. I have, actually. He assures me there is nothing going on. This is a subject I know a little something about, all right?

OTIS. Certainly.

KATE. Thank you.

(She puts earphones on.)

OTIS. *(Pause)* You've been talking to Carter, then? *(Pause)* I didn't realize. Thought I had the path to myself, but of course a lovely woman like yourself, bound to have suitors. Still, Carter. Like mating with a bull elephant seal. All very well for the moment, I suppose, but then off he waddles, a whole harem to attend to. Giselle in accounting, to mention just one. Not what you need, Kate. He does have youth on his side, of course, but youth is such a tawdry asset, don't you find? Any lout has his share. Now a man like myself, aged in the wood. Aged everywhere else, come to that. Still, if it's rampant lust you want, seek no further. After the wife passed on I thought the old boy was dead too, but since I met you, well, happy to report, he's not dead, only been recumbent. These last few weeks I've been like a man with three thighs. *(KATE looks up from her work, smiles at OTIS.)* See here, Kate, I want to say — Hear me all right, can you?

KATE. What?

(Removes earphones.)

OTIS. Hear me all right?
KATE. Yes, fine.

(Puts earphones back on.)

OTIS. Good. Been meaning to say …
KATE. What did you want to do tonight?
OTIS. Aha, well, yes, there's the thing …
KATE. Anything is fine with me.
OTIS. *(Softly)* Sure you can hear me? *(KATE concentrates on manuscript, can not hear him.)* Thought we'd make the beast with two backs, don't mean the camel, ha-ha. Bit of the old jolly roger. Bit of the soggy moss, eh?
KATE. *(Still viewing the manuscript.)* Anything at all is fine with me.
OTIS. Bend you over the sink, make barnyard sounds.
KATE. *(Studying script.)* I'm game for anything.
OTIS. Dress like a rooster, sing cock a doodle do.
KATE. How about seafood?
OTIS. Show you my giant squid, my dear. Put it on a platter with parsley and lemon, enough to serve a party of six.

(KATE looks up from manuscript again, smiles.)

KATE. You don't mind, do you?

(Removes earphones.)

OTIS. Whatever you want is fine with me, my dear.

KATE. *(Not looking up.)* You know, Otis, I've been meaning to tell you how very grateful I am for these dinners together. When I first came to the magazine I felt like such a stranger. You know what it's like, everyone has already formed relationships, no one is sure how to readjust things to take in an outsider — or even whether to take her in at all. It's like being adopted into a family when you're already an adult, they want you in some sense, or you wouldn't be there, but still ... and then you took me under your wing the way you did. It was so sweet, I can't tell you.

OTIS. Oh, well.

KATE. I was very touched. I am very touched.

OTIS. Not yet touched by me, let me point out. But then Mongo and I have hopes.

KATE. Do you know what I like best about you, Otis?

OTIS. Great steaming virility?

KATE. *(Removes earphones, looks up, turns to see OTIS behind her.)* What?

OTIS. What?

KATE. Did you say something?

OTIS. Good Lord, did I?

KATE. Something about virility?

OTIS. Ah. Senility. Said I was fast approaching it. Ha-ha.

KATE. You mustn't say that about yourself. People will take you seriously ... Do you know what I like most about you?

OTIS. Host of choices, eh?

KATE. I like the fact that you are so understanding. You don't want anything from me. That's so unusual in a man. Most of them are — well, you know what they're like.

OTIS. The swine.

KATE. But you're different. I don't know if that's because of your age or if you're just a genuinely decent, gentle man.

OTIS. Age?

KATE. Well, you know what I mean.

OTIS. Still a bit of steam in the boiler, you know.

KATE. I don't mean that you're old. But I do like maturity in a man.

OTIS. Wisdom of the years. Rock of ages, cleft for me.

KATE. Roger, for instance.

OTIS. Roger?

KATE. My ex-husband.

OTIS. Thought his name was Dickie, for some reason.

KATE. My ex-husband, who I am certain was named Roger, was one of those men who just never grow up. You know what I mean.

OTIS. Certainly. Never grow up. See it all the time. Must be a curse.

KATE. That's putting it mildly. It's like being married to a child.

OTIS. Poor thing. Must play hob with the psyche.

KATE. Well, the psyche is the whole problem, isn't it?

OTIS. That and the clothes, I should think.

KATE. The clothes?

OTIS. Hard to find them?

KATE. The clothes?

OTIS. How short was he?

KATE. About six feet.

OTIS. Well, there you have it, damned near impossible to find a suit to fit a man — six feet? You call that short?

KATE. No. I don't call that short.

OTIS. See here, you told me Dickie never grew up.

KATE. I meant he never matured.

OTIS. Oh. Thought you'd married a pygmy. Well, that's broad-minded of her, I said. A lesson to us all. Still, didn't work out, did it? Cultural conflicts, that sort of thing. Always dicey, so many differences. Where to live? In town? In the bush? What of the children? A brave woman to take on all those problems. Had to have been true love in the beginning. Blinds us all, love does. Heat of passion, pumping of the heart, blood pounding in the ears, hard to tell the forest for the trees in that state. Or, in the case of your pygmy, hard to tell the rain forest for the trees.

KATE. Otis.

OTIS. Yes, my dear.

KATE. I did not marry a pygmy. I married an Italian. He was not stunted in growth. He was emotionally immature.

OTIS. I quite understand, have the whole picture now. *(Pause)* No language problem?

KATE. An Italian American. He was semi-fluent — if you count hand gestures ... Weren't we talking about something?

OTIS. Weren't we?

KATE. I thought we were.

OTIS. Could have sworn it. Heard voices, that sort of thing.

KATE. Oh, yes. I was telling you how much these dinners have meant to me.

OTIS. Have they really?

KATE. You've been so kind, so gentle, so patient, I know I did an enormous amount of whining in the beginning.

OTIS. Not at all. I loved listening to you.

KATE. You must have been pretty fed up with my divorce and all of that.

OTIS. Just wanted to help you, my dear.

KATE. Well, you did, and I'm very grateful. I went through an awful lot of anxiety at first, coming back into the work force after all these years, exorcising Dickie, trying to fit into the family at the office.

OTIS. You fit in marvelously, scads of friends, all of that.

KATE. Not really scads.

OTIS. All the men talk about you.

KATE. I'm not interested in that ... Do they, really?

OTIS. Pretty woman, bright, friendly, single. Well, more than pretty, quite beautiful really.

KATE. Otis, are you blushing?

OTIS. Shy, you know, despite the poise.

KATE. I haven't seen a man blush since I was a teenager. I didn't know they could. I thought the blood was always rushing somewhere else.

OTIS. What? Yes, I see!

KATE. I don't really have scads of friends, you know. I'm friendly with a lot of people at the office, but that's not the same. I don't actually like very many of them. I'm just trying to get along. Is that horribly hypocritical of me?

OTIS. I understand perfectly.

KATE. How could you? You get along so easily with everyone.

OTIS. Me? Not at all.

KATE. I see you just chattering away all the time.

OTIS. Chattering, yes. Can't stand the silence, you see.

KATE. Really?

OTIS. Dread it. Two people standing there, nothing to say, awkward as a — how do you say, big beast, famously awkward, looks like ...

KATE. It doesn't matter.

OTIS. Quite right. Hate those silences, make me nervous as a, uh, thing. Except with the wife. I could be silent with her, very comfortable with her. Seemed to know what we were thinking without all the constant dithering. She'd just give me a touch, calm me down like a man with a dog. Amazing what a human touch can do.

KATE. You were very lucky in your marriage, Otis.

OTIS. Blessed. Didn't always appreciate it at the time.

KATE. Do you think of her a lot?

OTIS. The wife? ... Ruth ... Ruthie ... Miss her ... Miss her ... Miss her.

KATE. *(Pause)* Isn't it wonderful that we can talk this way to each other? I've always felt I could talk to you, I don't know why, but I just trusted you right from the beginning. There are so few men a woman can really, really talk to. And at the office, there's only you and Billy.

OTIS. Billy?

KATE. Billy in the art department? With the dyed blond hair?

OTIS. La de da Billy? See here, Kate, you're not suggesting that Billy and I, I and Billy ...

KATE. You share that wonderful quality of really listening to a woman.

OTIS. Oh, yes?

KATE. It's a sensitivity to the pain of others that men just don't have. They're always thinking of themselves and how they can get you into bed.

OTIS. The animals.

KATE. But not you, Otis.

OTIS. No, no.

KATE. Nor Billy.

OTIS. See here, about Billy ...

KATE. One of the things I've discovered since the divorce is how badly I need someone who understands me. Roger didn't understand me, he made no attempt to understand me, he didn't want to understand me, he just wasn't interested ... But I need someone who can understand me right down to my core. My soul cries out for understanding. I can't live without it anymore ...

OTIS. I understand you, Kate.

KATE. I believe you do, a little. And do you know why? I've discovered it's the outsiders of this world who care the most. Those who have been rejected by society — just as I was rejected by Roger. The people whose souls have been seared by pain and humiliation — those are the people who can really give love to others in pain.

OTIS. Seared like a rump steak myself.

KATE. This society is so cruel to anyone who doesn't fit into the mold. Well, I don't fit. It took me years and years to realize it, but I know it now, I don't fit either.

OTIS. Me neither.

KATE. Do you feel that way, too?

OTIS. Been a square peg all my life.

KATE. Really?

OTIS. Couldn't be more of a misfit. Just like that man in the movie. Who-do-call-him, with the mustache. Oh, you know, ears sticking out like tree mushrooms. "Damn you, Scarlet," something like that.

KATE. You do know what I'm talking about, don't you, Otis?

OTIS. *(He doesn't, but he covers.)* Ahhh ...

KATE. The sense of not being one of the mainstream.

OTIS. Quite. Complete black sheep, myself.

KATE. And why I have such a good rapport with Billy.

OTIS. Just to clear up the Billy business. Wouldn't want you to think our connection is all that close. Billy is essentially of a different persuasion, if you follow. I may have had the odd encounter as a youth, early confusion, any port in a storm, that sort of thing; once in a while in a circle, several of the fellows. No kissing, though, thinking all the while of Virginia Mayo, of course. Mind firmly fixed there, no question. All boys, oddly macho sort of thing, actually. And there was the time with the roommate in college, hardly counts, terribly drunk.

KATE. *(Kisses him lightly.)* Thank you, Otis.

OTIS. *(Rises, anticipating more.)* Ah, well ...

KATE. I came to work for the magazine and felt as if I didn't have a friend in the world but over the past few weeks I've come to realize I have a very special friend indeed.

OTIS. More than a friend, my dear.

KATE. Yes, much more than a friend.

OTIS. More of a soulmate.

KATE. Do you feel that way, too?

OTIS. Been wanting to tell you. Fair bursting with it.

KATE. Then I don't need to explain to you.

OTIS. Say no more. I understand completely.

KATE. I'm so glad.

OTIS. I'm a very happy man, my dear. *(OTIS embraces her. She hugs him back.)* I have something in my pocket for you, my dear.

KATE. It started so simply. Just a few friendly meals together. It all seemed so natural.

OTIS. Perfectly natural.

KATE. So natural. Then I realized I began to feel something. I was so surprised. After the divorce and everything.

OTIS. Yes.

KATE. You think you'll never feel anything again, certainly never want to get involved with anyone again. And then this of all things.

OTIS. Damned surprising.

KATE. I tried to fight it, of course.

OTIS. Give in to the heart.

KATE. But not to this.

OTIS. Why not?

KATE. It seemed so odd.

OTIS. Now, see here. Not all that odd.

KATE. I mean the sexual aspects of it.

OTIS. Nothing odd there. Spiritual affinity with Billy aside, I'm a screaming hetero, you know. Have the bona fides, two daughters, Karen and um, oh, um, lovely child ...

KATE. And I had been so angry at men.

OTIS. Perfectly justified. Pack of rotters.

KATE. *(Kisses him lightly.)* So I just want to say thank you. For being so sweet, for being so kind. For everything. Just for being you, Otis, whatever that is ... People will talk, of course.

OTIS. Let them and be damned to them.

KATE. You won't mind then?

OTIS. Why should I?

KATE. You won't be embarrassed by me?

OTIS. On the contrary! Proud as a — um — the bird, the bird ...

KATE. And you'll still be my friend?

OTIS. Bit more than that, I should say.

KATE. When you think about it, women with women just makes more sense.

OTIS. Women with women?

KATE. I've tried to get along with men all my life. They're just so much trouble.

OTIS. I seem to have lost the thread a bit. Women with women is intriguing, of course, can't deny it. But I thought at first, something a little more straight forward. Always time for a guest later, I suppose. The wife liked a bit of the thing with the oranges and the blindfold — what do you call that —

KATE. What are you talking about?

OTIS. Where one of you hides in the closet, the other has a blindfold and a handful of oranges ... you don't know that one?

KATE. It's not really about that, though, is it?

OTIS. What? No. Perfectly right.

KATE. It's about basic human communication.

OTIS. Quite right.

KATE. It's about I love you and you love me, and what do we do about it.

OTIS. *(Goes to one knee.)* By God, Kate, straight to the point. You shame me with your directness.

KATE. Why are you on the floor?

OTIS. See here, Kate, I had a speech prepared but can't remember it now anyway. The thing is, I'm lonely, you know. Want someone in my life. Don't want to carry on about it, but ... nights are hellish. Get a little frightened sleeping alone ... strange, isn't it, a man my age? Afraid of the dark. Well, not the dark, just the — emptiness.

Like a monster waiting for me, all that time alone ... See here, not very romantic that. The point is, as you put it, you love me and I love you and damn it, I say, let's get married and put an end to it.

KATE. *(Long pause.)* Otis ... you haven't been listening to me, have you?

OTIS. Listening like a hawk.

KATE. But ... I've been trying to tell you. I love you — but not in that way. I'm in love with someone else.

OTIS. Carter, that Spanish fly?

KATE. Not Carter. I love Giselle.

OTIS. Giselle?

KATE. Yes. Giselle.

OTIS. Giselle in accounting? The one with the ... ?

KATE. With the what?

OTIS. See here, correct me if I'm wrong — don't want to belabor the obvious, but damn it, Giselle's a woman.

KATE. Yes.

OTIS. As are you.

KATE. Yes.

OTIS. Well there you have it then. Need I say more?

KATE. All my life what I had been looking for was a man with the sensitivity of a woman. Someone I could really talk to, really trust, a man with whom I could share my tears and my fears the way I could with my girl friends. Then I finally realized, if it was the sensitivity of a woman I was after, why look for it in a man? Oh, Otis, it just makes so much sense, don't you see?

OTIS. Can't say that I do, damn it. Not really part of nature's grand design, you know. Puts a real short circuit in the procreation business.

KATE. It's not about child-bearing. It's about warmth and understanding and affection. Do you know any straight man who can give a woman affection without expecting it to turn into sex?

OTIS. That's the whole point, isn't it?

KATE. Not for a woman.

OTIS. Don't know how Carter is going to take this, he has his cap set for Giselle himself. *(Amused)* Makes him a bit of a fool, doesn't it? Chasing around after a ... *(Realizes)* Best be going on home, then. Sorry to have wasted your time.

KATE. Don't go.

OTIS. It's the best thing. Just toddle on off.

KATE. Why must you go?

OTIS. Damned embarrassed, that's why! You played me for a fool, Kate! Used me, led me on, treated me like a clown.

KATE. Oh, no ...

OTIS. Yes, by God. I know I appear something of the buffoon to some, but I have my feelings, I do, I have them and you've just ripped them up, Kate. Don't appreciate it, don't appreciate it at all.

KATE. Because I love someone else?

OTIS. Because of who you love! See here, if that's how you felt, why'd you let me carry on the way I did? All those dinners ...

KATE. I thought you liked me, I thought you liked being with me.

OTIS. I did, damn it. More the fool, I. Must say you've repaid my affection with a bit of sand in the eye.

KATE. Otis, please ... Don't leave.

OTIS. Why not?

KATE. I need you.

OTIS. No longer, it seems.

KATE. I need you now more than ever. Do you know what my life is going to be like when people know about Giselle? Who will be my friend then?

OTIS. Giselle and Billy, I should think.

KATE. That's not enough. I still want a complete life. I don't want to cut myself off from that world. I want to see things through your eyes, too.

OTIS. You want me as some sort of peephole on the world.

KATE. It's more than that ... I like you, Otis. I genuinely like you. You're sweet and kind and silly ...

OTIS. You want to use me!

KATE. Haven't you been using me?

OTIS. No, by God, I hadn't got around to it yet.

(Starts off.)

KATE. Otis, stay!

OTIS. What do I get out of it?
KATE. You won't be lonely anymore.
OTIS. Lonely? I'm not lonely.

(OTIS storms out.)

KATE. Then go on and to hell with you!

(Pause. OTIS returns.)

OTIS. See here, not fair, what you're asking. Asking me to be what do you call it.
KATE. Otis, we're not children. There's more than one way to get through life. Help me, stay with me, be my friend. Not my suitor, just my friend.
OTIS. Friends with a woman? Never done that, actually.
KATE. You were friends with your wife, weren't you?
OTIS. Ruthie? My best friend. Maybe my only real friend my whole adult life.
KATE. And was that just because of sex?
OTIS. Oh, no.
KATE. In fact, how much actual sex was there after the first few years?
OTIS. What? What are you implying? We went at it like rodents ...
KATE. *(Softly)* Otis.
OTIS. Not terribly much, actually.
KATE. You just liked being with her.
OTIS. Loved her.
KATE. Can't you keep liking me? Please? Can't we keep on with the dinners, the talks?
OTIS. To what end?
KATE. As an end in itself. Just friendship.
OTIS. *(Pause. Contemplatively.)* Friends with a woman.
KATE. *(Pause. Contemplatively.)* Friends with a man.
OTIS. What an unusual concept.
KATE. You've been doing it with me for weeks.

OTIS. But always with the prospect of the old rumdy-rum somewhere in the future. Makes a man tolerant of all kinds of twaddle if he thinks there's a payoff ... None of the old two-backed goolagong?

KATE. No.

OTIS. No possibility?

KATE. None.

OTIS. *(Pause)* Bit of relief, that. Not really my long suit. Never sure I had quite the right spot — didn't want to ask, seemed rather personal. *(Pause)* Just friendship. Could be interesting. Never one to shy from a challenge myself. Bit of a what's-his-name in my youth. Bring-em-back-alive type, into the savannah, armed only with a loyal native, Frank something, oh, it's an animal, the one with the thingums, what do you call that.

(She touches him.)

KATE. *(Soothingly)* Otis, I understand.

OTIS. Do you?

KATE. Yes, I do.

(A slow smile suffuses his face and he is at peace.)
(Curtain)

THE END

TRIANGLES FOR TWO

(SCENE: The same as preceding plays.)
(AT RISE: HE is looking out the window, peering at something in the distance. HE is alone on stage for a moment. His attitude gradually changes from curiosity to reflection. SHE enters quietly, watches him for a moment.)

SHE. I'm almost ready.

HE. *(Startled, thus angry.)* What are you doing, sneaking around like that?

SHE. Sorry if I frightened you.

HE. I wasn't frightened.

(HE returns his attention to the window.)

SHE. Do I look too sexy for the occasion?

(SHE pirouettes to show off her outfit.)

HE. *(Absently)* No.

SHE. Do I look sexy at all?

HE. No, you look fine ... They've hired a gardener now. *(SHE crosses to look out window.)* How can they afford that? How can everybody we know afford every damn thing they want while we're so deep in debt we can't see over it?

SHE. Why do you suppose they need a gardener?

HE. To trim the hedges, apparently. I don't understand it, I just don't get it. He doesn't make any more money than I do, but he spends like an Arab. If we go over there we'll probably find he's hired a butler.

SHE. How do you know he doesn't make more money than you do?

HE. Because he doesn't. He must plan on coming into an inheritance or something.

SHE. Maybe she has money. She acts like she comes from money. She's very refined.

HE. Refined? Refined? You call that refined?

SHE. I sense some pressure not to. How would you describe her.

HE. Affected. Snooty. I always feel like she's going to correct my grammar.

SHE. Always?

HE. What?

SHE. You said you always feel that way. Do you talk to her a lot?

HE. Just that once, when we had them over, right after they moved in.

SHE. Oh. It sounded like ...

HE. Have you been talking to them?

SHE. No ... We wave sometimes ... She seems nice.

HE. She can't very well correct your wave, can she?

SHE. He seems a little more distant.

HE. Thank God for that. I don't want to get anywhere near him. He gives me the creeps.

SHE. Maybe we should make more of an effort to get to know them.

HE. We made an effort. We had them over for drinks, didn't we?

SHE. That was five years ago.

HE. Let them make the effort. We were here first ... Oh, here comes his lordship now. A little gardening conference, no doubt.

SHE. He's rather attractive, isn't he?

HE. That stiff? He looks like a glass of iced tea.

SHE. I meant the gardener.

HE. *(Studies gardener.)* What is he wearing, a hair shirt? Looks like a gorilla.

(Pause. They are noticed by the neighbors. They both wave cheerfully.)

SHE. Hi! Hi!

HE. *(Waving)* Is that a backhoe? Jesus! Where does everybody else get the money?

SHE. *(Waving)* Beautiful evening … I said, "beautiful evening!"

HE. *(Steps away.)* Come away from there. Look at them staring at us. I feel like I'm being spied on in my own house. We have to build a fence.

SHE. Sometimes I feel as if they're living in our house — or we're living in theirs. Do you ever feel that?

HE. How can he afford a backhoe? We can't even get the floor redone.

SHE. What's the matter with the floor?

HE. It looks like someone's been walking over it with cleats. Look at that gouge. When did that happen?

SHE. It's only been there for ten years.

HE. It has? Looks like someone took a pick ax to it.

SHE. You don't remember what happened?

HE. Uh … not really.

SHE. It was Halloween, little Dickie was dressed as a cowboy and he was using your golf club as a horse and you came in with the hedge clippers and yelled "not with my 8-iron!" and his spurs got tangled up and the golf club knocked the hedge clippers … I can't believe you don't remember that.

HE. Oh, yeah.

SHE. What *do* you remember out of the last twenty years?

HE. I don't get bogged down in details, I remember the big picture.

SHE. Birth, death, golf scores? That sort of thing?

HE. Well, I don't remember what I was wearing on on our first date, if that's what you mean.

SHE. Bell bottoms, a gold chain and a magenta body shirt open halfway to your navel … And I thought you looked cute, in a hopelessly out-of-it sort of way.

HE. Just cute, huh? Not ruggedly handsome?

SHE. Magenta's not your color.

(SHE looks out the window, contemplatively.)

HE. What?
SHE. Nothing.

HE. I can always tell when you're thinking.

SHE. That's not hard. I'm always thinking.

HE. What did I do now?

SHE. Honey, do you ever wonder what it's like over there? In their house?

HE. No.

SHE. Don't you ever wonder what their life is like? They seem happy together. How do they do it?

HE. I just wonder how they can afford it.

SHE. Don't you wonder, when you see people sitting together in the movies and he puts his arm around her; or when they're walking and he holds her hand. Don't you ever wonder about them? Aren't you curious about their lives, what they do to stay together, how they manage to still feel that way?

HE. I put my arm around you in the movies. *(SHE is silent.)* Or I would if we ever went to the movies anymore ... I do ... You don't expect me to put my arm around you when we're watching television, do you? *(SHE looks at him, looks back at window.)* It's an entirely different medium ... Believe me, none of these goons you're talking about are any happier than we are.

SHE. Maybe you're right.

HE. You bet I'm right. Can you think of any couple you'd call happy — present company excepted, of course?

SHE. Of course ... Tina and Tom are happy.

HE. Tom is an alcoholic. He doesn't know if he's happy or not.

SHE. The Lapollas. They're always so perky.

HE. A pair of cheerleaders. Give them some pom-poms and they'll have us on our feet doing the wave ... Besides, he's having an affair.

SHE. No.

HE. He was seen with her in a restaurant in Greenwich.

SHE. I don't believe it. Tony Lapolla?

HE. With a girl who works in the booth at the drive-in photo place.

SHE. Poor Mary Lou.

HE. I feel sorry for the girl at the drive-in. Can you imagine making love with Tony Lapolla cheering you on?

SHE. *(Pause; quietly.)* Yes.

HE. What?

SHE. I see your point …

HE. Face it, we're as good as it gets. You and I are the last happy couple in America.

SHE. How do we do it?

(HE studies HER a moment to see how sarcastic that remark was.)

HE. We know our limitations. We don't look for more than we have, we're content with what we've got.

SHE. You never secretly want something else? I mean honestly now.

HE. What would I want?

SHE. You never yearn for — oh, I don't know — someone exotic, a house in Tahiti, something, anything, better. Maybe not even better, just different.

HE. You mean, do I secretly want a 24-year-old blonde with legs so long they could wrap around me twice and an ass as tight as a hospital bedsheet? Never, I love you just the way you are.

SHE. You can be very cruel.

HE. It's a joke! A joke! You brought it up, I was just teasing you.

SHE. Sometimes I think you don't like me at all.

HE. Don't be crazy, sweetheart. Of course I like you.

SHE. Of course.

HE. We're married.

SHE. I see. You'd better get ready if we're going to be there on time.

HE. Do we have to go? I don't want to see those people tonight.

SHE. What do you mean, "those people." They're our friends. You like them.

HE. Who's going to be there I like?

SHE. You like Murray.

HE. Murray is such a negative son-of-a-bitch. Have you ever heard him say anything nice about anybody?

SHE. … Otis will be there.

HE. Otis has the attention span of a newt.

SHE. I think he's rather sweet. Most women do.

HE. Last time I saw him we were talking about the Red Sox and the next thing I know he's going on about the growing lesbian population.

SHE. I like that woman he's with. Kate?

HE. How does he do it?

SHE. There's something, I don't know, very appealing about her. Something different.

HE. I've noticed.

SHE. You have?

HE. ... Not particularly ... Seriously, sweetheart, do we really have to go to this thing?

SHE. These are our friends. Friendship has certain requirements. One of them is that you act friendly now and again. You don't have to mean it.

HE. I can't deal with that hypocrisy — I don't like those people.

SHE. You don't have to like your friends. Just be sociable. If it was up to you we'd have no social life at all.

HE. Nobody ever talks about anything. All I hear is "how's your mother, mine too, I love your dress." Every time I try to raise a topic everyone shies away from me as if I passed gas.

SHE. Poor baby. What did you want to talk about?

HE. I don't care, the death penalty, the politics of AIDS, anything besides ornamental shrubs. The only time anything *sincere* is said is when we're standing in the doorway on our way out. Then we can't exchange *enough* information, but that's just because we're all relieved we're going home.

SHE. I didn't know you were interested in the politics of AIDS.

HE. Of course I am, I'm an informed citizen.

SHE. What is the politics of AIDS?

HE. Are. What *are* the politics of AIDS.

SHE. Is. So what are they?

HE. Believe me, it's nothing you want to talk about.

SHE. I saw you chatting with Richard for a full hour at the last party. You looked absolutely engrossed, you never left the spot.

HE. I was comatose. I was so bored I screwed my toes into the floor.

SHE. What were you talking about?

HE. Curling.

SHE. Curling? With the ice and the broom? What do you know about curling?

HE. Nothing. I was faking it.

SHE. Why?

HE. A man can never admit to an ignorance of sport. Might as well wear a dress.

SHE. Why didn't you change the subject?

HE. If we didn't talk about sports, we wouldn't be able to talk at all. And that was Roger I was talking to, not Richard.

SHE. I thought it was Richard.

HE. Richard doesn't know anything about curling, he's into shooting.

SHE. I thought that was Roger.

HE. How little you know.

SHE. If you're so bored talking to men, why don't you join the women? We have interesting conversations.

HE. Women don't have conversations, they just sit around and *agree* with each other. "Oh, I know, I know, I know." Conversation requires a difference of opinion.

SHE. You're thinking of debate. If you men would stop competing you might enjoy talking to each other. Being sympathetic is how you learn things.

HE. I've heard your meaningful conversations with Marian. "What did you wear and what did you wear and what did he say and what did she say."

SHE. That's when men are around. We talk about other things when you're not there.

HE. Like what?

SHE. We talk about men.

HE. Really? What do you say about us?

SHE. Anything. Everything. Whatever we feel. We talk about our fantasies for one thing.

HE. You're kidding. Really?

SHE. Really.

HE. What's Marian's fantasy?

SHE. Sex with a hairless man.

HE. That lets out Murray. He's hairy as a werewolf.

SHE. And you. I told her you have hair on your back.

HE. Why did you tell her that, for Christ's sake?

SHE. Because we were talking about our men.

HE. Don't you think that's just a little bit personal?

SHE. That's the point of intimate conversation.

HE. It's supposed to be personal about *you*, not me. I would no more talk about you like that — they could pull my tongue out first — I can't believe you discuss us that way.

SHE. Oh, men don't talk about us, I suppose.

HE. The only time I ever mentioned you to Murray I complained that you were always late. He said, "Women." End of conversation. Does that classify as intimate?

SHE. I'm not always late.

HE. What else did you tell her about me?

SHE. I forget.

HE. Women never forget anything. Did you tell her anything else about ... my body?

SHE. We're not really as concerned about that part of you as you men think.

HE. Yeah? You don't ... compare?

SHE. We *notice*, but it's not an obsession. Marian said Murray hasn't made love to her in three months.

HE. She *told* you that?

SHE. I'm her friend, who else should she tell?

HE. She might start with Murray.

SHE. Murray already knows. Besides, she can't talk to Murray.

HE. *(Gleefully)* Is he impotent?

SHE. She's afraid he just isn't attracted to her anymore.

HE. Why wouldn't he be? Marian's a damned attractive woman.

SHE. I thought you didn't like her.

HE. Marian? Of course I like her. And I feel sorry for her, married to Murray. She deserves someone who would appreciate her.

SHE. Who did you have in mind?

HE. So old Murray's impotent. That's great! *(Laughs)* Oh, that bag of wind. No wonder he's so aggressive everywhere else.

SHE. Lots of men your age have episodes of impotence.

HE. Well, episodes, sure, episodes. That's perfectly normal, nothing wrong with that, perfectly normal, doesn't mean a thing. Now and then. Once in a while.

SHE. Sometimes.

HE. Occasionally. A guy doesn't always feel like it. But not three months. We're not like women.

SHE. What do you mean, you're not like women?

HE. Well, we've got the stronger sex drive. We may not always be up to it, because, let's face it, more is required of a man, but we're always thinking about it, we're *psychologically* prepared.

SHE. I think about sex all the time, so does Marian. So do most of the women I know.

HE. No. That's not true.

SHE. At home, in the car, at work, at the supermarket.

HE. You never told me that. Women? You're kidding.

SHE. Only a little.

HE. Who do you think about having it with?

SHE. Various men.

HE. Stop.

SHE. The gardener. John Cleese. Murray's accountant with the sad eyes.

HE. He's gay.

SHE. Until he meets me.

HE. I get it. You're talking about swooning and candle light dinners and nursing an invalid back to health and all those romance novel things.

SHE. I'm talking about if-he-says-fuck-I'll-beat-him-to-the-floor kind of sex.

HE. I had no idea it was so important to you.

SHE. I know.

HE. Why didn't you ever tell me this?

SHE. It's not something we talk about. I assumed you knew.

HE. How would I know that? I thought women had to be wooed into having sex.

SHE. Into *having sex*, maybe, not into thinking about it.

HE. What … I'm afraid to ask this now. When you and Marian swapped fantasies — what was your fantasy?

SHE. To have sex with a man who puts his arm around me.

HE. Are you getting at me for something? Because of that remark about the 25-year-old? That was a joke!

SHE. You said she was 24. Or do you know more than one blonde with legs so long they'll wrap around you twice?

HE. I don't remember what I said. It wasn't important.

SHE. I do. It was … But apparently sex is more important to me than to you.

HE. It hasn't been that long.

SHE. Four weeks.

HE. It hasn't been four weeks. Maybe a week. Ten days, tops.

SHE. June sixth.

HE. I had a cold, I didn't want to infect you.

SHE. The cold was three weeks ago.

HE. I need recovery time … If you wanted it so bad, you have to let me *know*.

SHE. Last night, I squeezed you when you were brushing your teeth.

HE. I thought you were just trying to get past.

SHE. Then when you were reading in bed, I tickled your arm.

HE. Yeah, but you weren't wearing your purple number. You had on the torn flannel and the white socks so I thought you were just trying to annoy me.

SHE. Sometimes I think you don't like me at all.

HE. Come on, I'll show you how much I like you.

SHE. Sure, now, when we don't have any time.

HE. We've got all night. We won't go to the party. I don't need a social life. I've got you.

SHE. But what have I got? … I have to have other people in my life. I'm not like you. I don't know how you men do it.

HE. Do what?

SHE. Live without friends.

HE. I have friends. I have plenty of friends.

SHE. Who?

HE. You want me to *name* them?

SHE. That way I'll know who they are.

HE. Sten.

SHE. You work with Sten.

HE. So? He's a work friend. How about Greg?

SHE. You play golf with Greg.

HE. He's a golf friend. That doesn't mean he's not my friend.

SHE. What do you talk to him about?

HE. Golf ... and other things.

SHE. What are the names of his children?

HE. Huey, Dewey and Louie. I don't know. That's not what we talk about.

SHE. You don't have friends, you have categories.

HE. ... Murray. Murray's my friend. All purpose.

SHE. You just said Murray was a son-of-a-bitch.

HE. I don't happen to want to spend time with him, but Murray and I go way back.

SHE. You only see him because he's married to my friend, Marian. Do you have any friends you talk to? That's the measure of a friend, isn't it?

HE. I have friends I don't have to talk to. That's the measure of a friend.

SHE. The difference being, it's very difficult to tell your kind of friend from a stranger.

HE. I'll tell you what a friend is. If you're climbing a mountain and hanging by a rope, who do you want on the other end of that rope? How many friends do you have you can rely on like that?

SHE. So few, since I left the Alps.

HE. A friend is someone you can count on in extremis. You may never see him, you may never talk to him, you might lose all communication, not even know where he lives or if he's still alive, but if you need him, he'll be there.

SHE. Sort of like Tinkerbell? Do you have anyone you talk to *intimately*?

HE. Oh, the big buzz word. What do you mean by 'intimately'?

SHE. Something beyond "Don't let go of the rope!" If you had a problem — I don't mean a business problem, I don't mean a golf swing problem — a personal problem — which one of your friends would you talk to about it?

HE. Define "problem."

SHE. A marital problem.

HE. *(Pause)* Hypothetically, right?

SHE. Say you were feeling depressed and frightened about your marriage. Which of your friends would you talk to about it? Greg? Sten? Murray?

HE. I wouldn't tell any of those bastards.

SHE. Why not?

HE. I wouldn't give them the satisfaction. They're not that kind of friend.

SHE. Who is?

HE. ... Fortunately I don't have a marital problem ... All right, give me a minute, I'll tell you who I'd talk to in a crisis. *(Long pause.)* God, this is depressing. And I'm a popular guy. When I was in school I had lots of buddies, we could talk about anything ... It's your fault, you know.

SHE. My fault.

HE. I got married. I entered the world of women. Gay guys have friends, single guys have friends, but married men, oh no, they're at home with their wives.

SHE. You see no one, you talk to no one, and this is my fault.

HE. You made me a householder and a babysitter.

SHE. I inflicted a home on you. I forced you to have a family. I gave you a place in the community.

HE. These are woman things.

SHE. No wonder you resent it ... You could be rappelling down Mt. Everest right now ... Maybe men and women shouldn't marry in the first place. We seem to have no natural affinity for it.

HE. That's it! Kids start segregating by instinct in the second grade. We don't even speak the same language.

SHE. Oh, it's the same language. Some of us just aren't listening. I'm going to the party.

HE. What about me?

SHE. This will be perfect for you. You don't have to leave the house, you don't have to talk to anyone. No friendship, no intimacy. You can practice coiling your rope. I'm going to be with my friends and have superficial conversations and have a wonderful time. *(SHE crosses, stops at window.)* What are they doing now?

HE. Digging a moat?

SHE. The gardener has something in a big garbage bag. He's putting it in the hole with a tree.

(HE joins her.)

HE. That's a hemlock.

SHE. It's a yew, actually. But he put the bag in first.

HE. Fertilizer.

SHE. Maybe, but he didn't open the bag. *(They stand and stare out the window for a moment.)* Are *they* a happy couple, do you think?

(HE puts his arm around her.)

HE. *We're* a happy couple. *(No response from her.)* If you're going to the party to be with your friends, I guess I'll go and be with my friend.

SHE. Who's that?

HE. I've only got one.

SHE. I know.

HE. You're my best friend in the whole world.

SHE. I know.

HE. *(Cajoling)* And who's your best friend, huh, who is he?

SHE. *(Pause)* Marian.

(Lights fade slowly as they continue to stare out the window.)
(Curtain)

THE END

CAPTIVATING ONE-ACT DRAMAS AND

Specks
ROB SHIMKO

Specks takes place in a diner on New Year's Eve. It is the story of three lonely people: a waitress named Molly, her possessive mother, and an obsessive-compulsive regular who makes intricate sculptures from his dishes. As they try in vain to have a party, a mysterious stranger from a real party across the street enters and triggers catastrophic changes in their lives. The stranger begins to seduce Molly and antagonize the others. The play builds to a fiery climax as Molly chooses between her old life and a new one with the stranger. 2 m., 2 f. (#21436)

Guarding the Bridge
CHUCK GORDON

A father and son occupy a broken-down bridge in a remote wooded area. It becomes apparent that the father is a manifestation of the son's memory from twenty years ago as he recalls events that occurred on the day Martin Luther King, Jr. was assassinated. Clay, the son, is well-educated while his father was an ignorant and bigoted farmer. As the play progresses, despite Clay's protests to the contrary, it becomes obvious that his father's bigotry is embedded in his subconscious. Structured as an extended monologue with occasional interruptions from the father, *Guarding the Bridge* is an analysis of the evolution of racism from father to son and, more importantly, its inherent roots in fear. 2 m. (#09949)

**Send for your copy of the Samuel French
BASIC CATALOGUE OF PLAYS AND MUSICALS**

COMEDIES FROM OUR CATALOGUE

Position Available
BRAD GROMELSKI

A classified ad for a personal secretary to novelist B. Wright draws Mel Shovanik and Grace Femino to the writer's door, where they are greeted by Betram, the butler. Mel thinks that Grace is the maid and she thinks that he is the novelist. They discover they are both after the job and become competitive. Then they realize Bertram is not a butler. In fact, he is not even Bertram. And Mel is not Mel. Nor is Grace Grace. Who are they? And who is B. Wright? After the mystery unravels there is still a position available. 2 m., 1 f. (#18232)

And Go to Innisfree
JANE LENOX TODDIE

It's October. The beach is deserted. A woman appears, flowered parasol raised and long skirt sweeping the sand. She has come to make a decision, but will she make it alone? The middle-aged matron she was argues for the comfort of a retirement home while the child she was urges her to sit again and eat blackberries, to lie under the brambles and study ants, and to arise at long last and go to Innisfree. This one-act drama is by the author of *White Room of My Remembering, Lookin' for a Better Berry Bush, A Bag of Green Apples, A Little Something for the Ducks, A Scent of Honeysuckle, Is That the Bus to Pittsburgh?* and other popular short plays. 3 f. (#3579)

**Send for your copy of the Samuel French
BASIC CATALOGUE OF PLAYS AND MUSICALS**

Off-Off-Broadway Festival

FOURTH SERIES
An Empty Space   Nothing Immediate   Open Admission

FIFTH SERIES
Batbrains   Me Too, Then!   "Hello, Ma!"

SIXTH SERIES
A Bench at the Edge   Seduction Duet

SEVENTH SERIES
MD 20/20   Passing Fancy

EIGHTH SERIES
Dreamboats   A Change from Routine   Auto-Erotic Misadventure

NINTH SERIES
Now Departing   Something to Eat   The Enchanted Mesa
The Dicks   Piece for an Audition

TENTH SERIES
Delta Triangle   Dispatches from Hell   Molly and James
Senior Prom   12:21 p.m.

ELEVENTH SERIES
Daddy's Home   Ghost Stories   Recensio   The Ties That Bind

TWELFTH SERIES
The Brannock Device   The Prettiest Girl in Lafayette
County   Slivovitz   Two and Twenty

THIRTEENTH SERIES
Beached   A Grave Encounter   No Problem   Reservations
for Two   Strawberry Preserves   What's a Girl to Do

FOURTEENTH SERIES
A Blind Date with Mary   Bums   Civilization and Its Mal-
contents   Do Over   Tradition 1A

FIFTEENTH SERIES
The Adventures of Captain Neato-Man   A Chance Meeting
Chateau Rene   Does This Woman Have a Name?   For
Anne   The Heartbreak Tour   The Pledge

SIXTEENTH SERIES
As Angels Watch   Autumn Leaves   Goods   King of the
Pekinese Yellowtail   Uranium   Way Deep   The Whole
Truth   The Winning Number

Plays from Samuel French

SEVENTEENTH SERIES
Correct Address   Cowboys, Indians and Waitresses   Homebound   The Road to Nineveh   Your Life Is a Feature Film

EIGHTEENTH SERIES
How Many to Tango?   Just Thinking   Last Exit Before Toll   Pasquini the Magnificent   Peace in Our Time   The Power and the Glory   Something Rotten in Denmark   Visiting Oliver

NINETEENTH SERIES
Awkward Silence   Cherry Blend with Vanilla   Family Names   Highwire   Nothing in Common   Pizza: A Love Story   The Spelling Bee

TWENTIETH SERIES
Pavane   The Art of Dating   Snow Stars   Life Comes to the Old Maid   The Appointment   A Winter Reunion

TWENTY-FIRST SERIES
Whoppers   Dolorosa Sanchez   At Land's End   In with Alma   With or Without You   Murmurs   Ballycastle

TWENTY-SECOND SERIES
Brothers   This Is How It Is   Because I Wanted to Say Tremulous   The Last Dance   For Tiger Lilies Out of Season.   The Most Perfect Day

TWENTY-THIRD SERIES
The Way to Miami   Harriet Tubman Visits a Therapist   Meridan, Mississippi   Studio Portrait   It's Okay, Honey   Francis Brick Needs No Introduction

TWENTY-FOURTH SERIES
The Last Cigarette   Flight of Fancy   Physical Therapy   Nothing in the World Like It   The Price You Pay   Pearls   Ophelia   A Significant Betrayal

TWENTY-FIFTH SERIES
Strawberry Fields   Six Inch Adjustable   Evening Education   Hot Rod   A Pink Cadillac Nightmare   East of the Sun and West of the Moon

American
igle canopy
rizzled vet-
d desire to
to recover

alerted by a
find his fa-
r to a small
City, close
rney through
nally distant
es of joy and

**PUBLISHED TOGETHER
IN A SAMUEL FRENCH ACTING EDITION**

Samuel French, Inc.
SERVING THE THEATRICAL COMMUNITY SINCE 1830